RISING ABOVE THE BATTLE SCARS

IF YOU CAN TAKE IT IN LIFE, YOU CAN MAKE IT

Rising Above the Battle Scars Copyright © 2018 Betty Thompson

ISBN: 978-1986704366

All rights reserved. No part of this publication may be reproduced, stored in a retrieval system, or transmitted, in any form or by any means, electronic, mechanical, photocopying, recording or otherwise, without the prior written permission of the publishers.

The author has made every effort to ensure the accuracy of the information within this book was correct at time of publication.

First edition: 2018

RISING ABOVE THE BATTLE SCARS

IF YOU CAN TAKE IT IN LIFE, YOU CAN MAKE IT

BY

BETTY L. THOMPSON

FOREWORD FROM CONGRESSWOMAN MAXINE WATERS

As a native of St. Louis, Missouri, I have known Betty Thompson for more than 40 years, and I can truly attest to one thing: **Betty is a fighter**.

Betty's fighting spirit led her from the housing projects of Carr Square Village to the Missouri State House. With her book, *Rising Above the Battle Scars*, Betty is providing a firsthand look at her strength, courage, and perseverance in the face of seemingly insurmountable odds.

Whether you are a single parent working two or three jobs, making minimum wage or less in order to put food on the table. Whether you have been exploited, harassed, or taken advantage of in your personal or professional life. Whether you are suffering from an illness or disease and are worried about the future. Whether you have been disrespected or feel your talent is not appreciated or valued in the workplace -- Betty's story will inspire and encourage you to keep fighting because, "*You can make it.*"

DEDICATION PAGE

Dedicated to my beautiful and only daughter, Sonja M. Thompson-Branscomb.

ACKNOWLEDGMENTS

To my husband, Jack: For your love, friendship, patience, understanding and support, for the four amazing children and the fifty-eight wonderful years together, I love you and thank you from my heart.

To my son, Anthony "Tony" Thompson and daughter-in-law, Kim: Words can't express the emotions I feel for all of your help in turning my dream into a reality. From the top to the bottom of my heart, I love you both and I thank you.

To my son, Kwame and daughter, Sonja: A very special thank you goes out to you all as well, for your tireless efforts in making this book go from head to paper. I couldn't have done this without you. I love you and I thank you so much.

To my sister, Sandra Ella Stittum, thank you for helping me make this book possible.

To Samella Bolden, thank you for your help in pushing this book forward.

To my granddaughter, Kayla: I can't begin to thank you enough for all of the love, support, and help you poured into this project. Know that I love and appreciate you always.

To my close friend, mentor, someone that I admire and respect, Congresswoman Maxine Waters, it would take a whole book for me to truly thank you for all that you've done. It is truly an honor and privilege to know you.

ACKNOWLEDGMENT PAGES

To my husband, children, siblings and grandchildren, coworkers, political allies, friends, faithful supporters, and uplifting church members: thank you.

A special thank you goes to my sisters, Sandra Stittum and the late Rosemary Banner.

To my family and friends in the following places, I thank you: Martin, Tennessee; Memphis, Tennessee; New Jersey; Dallas, Texas; Florida; Oklahoma; Mississippi; Minnesota; Arizona; Chicago, Illinois; Seattle, Washington; Akron, Ohio; Las Vegas; Los Angeles, California; Maryland; Washington DC; and St. Louis, Missouri.

To the following foundations, organizations, associations and churches, thank you:

A special thank you goes to the 72nd Legislative District in Missouri: University City, Pagedale and Wellston, for believing in me and electing me to office.

The Kwame Foundation

The Kwame Building Group, Inc.

The Tyrone Thompson Nonviolent Institute

Head Start

YWCA

Mound City Bar Association

Dr. Martin Luther King Junior Missouri State Commissioners

Throwing and Growing Inc.

Dwaun J. Warmack, President of Harris-Stowe State University

Better Family Life

Human Development Corporation (HDC)

Michael Brown Foundation

Anthony Lamar Smith Foundation

Universal African People Foundation

Urban League of Metropolitan St. Louis

Coalition of 100 Black Women

Young Organized Political Committee (YOPAC)

National Council of Negro Women

Black Elected County Officials (BECO)

Dr. Robert and Ava Williams

Judge George and Judy Draper

Reverend Doctor Harold Butler of Northern Missionary Baptist Church and family

New Perfect Peace Church

Waymen AME Church

St. Luke's AME Church

Thank you to the following individuals: Patricia White Hamilton, Odessa Richardson, Attorney Annette Slack, Aileen Plump, Claudette Gibson, Rebecca Thompson-Willis, Alice Windom, Regina Dennis, Thelma Evans, Edna Foxworth, Ollie Stewart, Cleo Willis, Daisy Brumette, Margie Carter, Zakie Baruti, Anthony Shaheed.

Thank you to the following for assisting with the documentary:

Cinematographer: Alex Peterson, and his assistants, Chesney and Gary Stittum

Music provided by: Anthony "Tony" Thompson and T-Beats Studios

Wardrobe provided by: Henry Mason

Makeup: Ayanna and Imani Branscomb

TESTIMONIALS

Tom Irwin, President of Civic Progress

"I'd rather see a prayer than hear one." When he'd see me coming, he'd say, "When I worked with Betty, every day, I saw a prayer."

Hazel Erby, St. Louis County Council member, 1st District

"She was my mentor, I learned so much from her. She was also my neighbor and our children grew up together."

Pam Salami, Consultant in Dallas, TX

"I've never seen anybody as kind and patient as Ms. Betty."

Antoine Coffer, Council member in Phoenix, AZ

"Ms. Thompson's always willing to help. She's given me lots of helpful tips on handling the office."

Lewis Reed, President, St. Louis Board of Aldermen

"Betty is the mother of the St. Louis Civil Rights Movement."

Honorable Darlene Green, Controller, City of St. Louis

"I thank Betty for a lifetime of service in justice and equality."

Mayor Ted Hoskins, mayor of Berkley, MO

"In working with Betty, I have found her to be loyal and passionate about her work."

Honorable Mavis Thompson, License Collector, City of St. Louis

"I honor Betty for her lifetime of passion and service."

Sidney and Geraldine Clark

"We respect her; she's always kind, loving and warm. We often reminisce about family life when we get together."

Reverend Lloyd, Pastor of New Perfect Peace Church, St. Louis

"Betty always gives me good advice."

Sherry Maxwell, Program Assistant at Lincoln University, Charleston Outreach Center

"Ms. Betty has been a light for us in darkness and has provided hope when we didn't have hope. She's fearless and lives her testimony. And, the Bootheel of Missouri is better from knowing her."

Clarence Jackson, Executive Director of the Ecumenical Ministers Group & St. Louis County Business Man

"I call Betty, 'Boss Lady' Thompson. She knows how to take charge and does it with humility and kindness."

Kathy Osborne, Regional Business Council

"When I came to know Betty, it was like I'd met an angel."

Dorcel Caldwell

"As a young person growing up, I never met someone as passionate as Betty Thompson."

Joyce Buck, former principal in Normandy School District

"Betty L. Thompson is an advocate and humanitarian for people, always wanting the best for them. She believes people can and will do their best, if given the opportunity."

TABLE OF CONTENTS

FOREWORD FROM CONGRESSWOMAN MAXINE WATERS..........iv

DEDICATION PAGE...v

ACKNOWLEDGMENTS vi

ACKNOWLEDGMENT PAGES...viii

TESTIMONIALS...xi

CHAPTER 1: GROWING UP 1

CHAPTER 2: LIFE AS A YOUNG WOMAN............................17

CHAPTER 3: WIFE…MOTHER…FAMILY 27

CHAPTER 4: FINDING MY PURPOSE AND PASSION.....…39

CHAPTER 5: RUNNING FOR OFFICE 41

CHAPTER 6: HOW I DEAL WITH LIFE, THE UPS AND DOWNS.....71

CHAPTER 7: LOSING TYRONE AND TYRELL....................77

CHAPTER 8: MY MISSION TO EMPOWER THE COMMUNITY 87

CHAPTER 9: HOW TO STAY INVOLVED AS YOU GET OLDER.....91

FINAL THOUGHTS 97

CHAPTER 1

GROWING UP

My father, William Sam Sr. and mother, Lubirtha (Lacey) Bolden married at a very young age, and soon started their family in the small country town of Helm, Mississippi. Helm was so small; it only had three stores, four churches, and one elementary school for coloreds only. If there was a sick child or someone deathly ill, Billy Parker's trailer owners would spatter a bale of hay on the road and take the sick child and the mom to the nearest doctor, which was three towns away.

I was born into what would eventually become a large family. My parents had thirteen children in all, ten boys and three girls; coincidentally, my mother also came from a family with thirteen children. I was the fourth child and first girl my parents had, following William Sam Jr., Wardell, and Otis. Born prematurely on December 3rd, 1939, I weighed two pounds at birth. Not much was wagered on my chances of survival and being so small, I was given a shoebox for a makeshift bed. My delicate system was so fragile, from what I was told, I could only tolerate goat's milk for my formative years. In fact, I was told that people used to say that my parents should give up on me, but they didn't. They nurtured, loved and spoke life into me, and I thrived.

There was a lot of love in our house, but not a lot of money; we made do with what we had and were thankful though. Momma was sickly most of the time, while Daddy worked odd jobs to keep a roof over our heads and food on the table. Our family was made up of mostly farmers and their main crop was cotton. My mom's older brother, Mack, was very in-demand as a land surveyor. The white people in a several-town radius depended upon him for their land measurements, which extended a distinguished reputation to our family that was not afforded to many others. Because of Uncle Mack, our family was able to negotiate a shared land deal with many other landowners, which allowed each large family a measure of respectability and prosperity, also unheard of in those days. It was a fruitful joint venture that benefitted everyone, black and white alike.

Most of our family had a hankering for living life in the big city, so the adults held a meeting and everyone agreed it was time to give big city life a try. They set their sights on one of two cities and my paternal uncles decided to settle in Chicago, Illinois or St. Louis, Missouri. Uncle Moses was the only holdout. He had ten girls and four boys, and he wasn't convinced he wanted to go just yet. Although Uncle Moses had lost his wife during the childbirth of their fourth boy child, Sammy Lee, he liked how and where his children were growing up. He often told them, "Go on and test the big city water in St. Louis and if it turns out well, I'll join you." But, he never did; he remained in Mississippi with his children. Uncle Mack and Aunt Sarah, on the other hand, moved to Chicago and remained there. Aunt Sarah preceded him in death, and he lived until he was ninety-five years of age. Uncles Eli, Benny, Charlie, and my father decided on St. Louis.

I was only six months old when my father packed us up and moved us to St. Louis, where we lived with Mother's sister, my namesake Aunt Betty. We stayed there until an apartment in the Carr Square Village lower-income housing project was ready. In 1945, my family was one of the first families to move into our new place in Carr Square Village.

We adjusted quickly into family life at Carr Square, settling down and developing a comfortable routine. Big Mama decided to move to St. Louis to live with us. I was happy that Big Mama shared a bed with me. Sadly, she died in that same bed three and a half years later. This was the first time I'd ever experienced someone close to me in the family dying. We lost our grandmother, who we all loved and respected. Thinking back, I can remember feeling inconsolable, as if I had personally lost a part of me.

Life growing up in Carr Square Village had its ups and downs. I was surrounded by my loving family, having fun playing with my siblings and other kids. But still, sometimes the other kids would pick on me, because I always wore a bonnet, hat, or some type of scarf on my head. Wigs at that point were not an option; they were available only in Hollywood, a major city to the stars.

People, mostly children back then, would stop, laugh and point, stare and say, "Look, Mom, over there. That bald-headed girl has no hair. Mom, where is her hair?" Adults wouldn't say much, they'd just gesture discreetly and whisper among themselves. Nobody really says anything about a little boy not having hair, but when they see a little girl who has no hair, people tend to gawk, and little kids just make fun. You see, I was born with a condition called alopecia, meaning a total lack of body hair. At the time, my family and I didn't know there was a name for it; we just knew that I didn't have any hair. Surprisingly, out of all of my siblings, there were five of us who had alopecia. Two of my brothers had alopecia, while all three of us girls also had it. I can't recall if any other family members outside the immediate family had it.

My brothers were very protective of me and would always straighten out the kids who picked at me. I tried not to let it bother me, but deep down inside, my feelings would be hurt. Momma would always be right there to comfort me. My mother was a very loving and nurturing woman, and she was always my biggest influence. I admired Momma so much. I've always tried to model my life after hers.

Before I knew it, I was five years old and it was time to go to kindergarten. I looked forward to going to school with other kids and learning at the Carr School. However, I wound up transferring to Carr Lane School because some of the other kids would pick on me because I had no hair. They'd snatch my bonnet off and run off with it, saying mean things, like, "Ohhhh, look at her bald head." My brothers, who were very protective of me, would get my bonnet back and chase the mean kids away.

For the most part, things and life in general were going rather well for me, outside of the occasional teasing from kids who didn't understand my issue. Then one day, tragedy decided to introduce itself to my family again. Ms. Johnson, my teacher, told me to come with her and she brought me home because my first cousin, Willie Ernest, had died. While driving his boss out of town, he had an accident and was killed. My mother had just been talking to Willie Ernest when he had that accident. Needless to say, Momma was heartbroken, right along with the rest of us.

From an early age, I knew I wanted to be either a nurse or perhaps a missionary. Even back then, I loved to help people. Without even putting much thought into it, I had already aligned my steps to being successful at doing what I loved.

For most of my youth, I grew up in the close-knit confines of the Carr Square Village Housing Complex. The short name for our low-rise complex, was indeed properly named, "The Village," as we were like an African tribe. We were close like kin and looked out for one another like family. Back then, everyone looked out for each other, there wasn't any "looking the other way". Neighbors watched out for neighbors, the elders watched out for the children. Your neighbors were like surrogate parents and could scold your children, or the other neighbor's children if they got out of line. In turn, you could also chastise other neighbor's children. Children were kind and respectful to their elders back then, and paid attention when they were spoken to. You sure can't do that nowadays, it would create a huge problem. I've often wished that trend had continued into today's times. I truly think quite a few situations could be avoided by living by this credo.

Of course, in a small apartment with several growing children and two adults, it was quite crowded and the topic of moving came up quite a bit. The county was in the process of building new housing and soon, it was official. We were moving from Carr Square Village to our next residence; the newly-built, high-rise model named Pruitt-Igoe, one of the largest housing developments for lower income residents in the country.

Pruitt-Igoe, whose construction was completed in 1955, was named for two esteemed St. Louis residents; Wendell O. Pruitt, a black World War II fighter pilot and also a member of the legendary Tuskegee Airmen, and William L. Igoe, a former U.S. Congressman who represented St. Louis from 1913 - 1921. At first, P-I, as it was affectionately called, was supposed to be segregated housing. Pruitt Homes would house the African-American residents, and Igoe Apartments would be home for the white residents. However, this decision was shut down by a federal circuit judge and the P-I Projects would be integrated.

Standing proudly on the outskirts of downtown St. Louis, Pruitt-Igoe was a government housing project experiment, which became the premier model for our city, as well as other major metropolitan cities. P-I was thirty-three buildings with twelve floors, containing a total of 2,870 affordable apartments for tenants with low incomes. Designed by architect Minoru Yamasaki, who would later design the original World Trade Center, Pruitt-Igoe's buildings contained what were called skip-stop elevators. These elevators didn't stop on every floor, meaning that the elevators only served the first, fourth, seventh and tenth floors. Tenants who lived on non-stop floors had to use the stairs. This was supposed to ease congestion on the elevators. The floors with elevator stops had large common areas, laundry rooms, and garbage chutes.

The projects, designed with large families such as ours in mind, made us among the first to move to the new eleven-story, brick high-rise, along with four other large families like ours. The complex offered three to five bedrooms, all with one full bath and a convenient half-bath near the front of the apartment; amenities uncommon to public housing.

I remember the excitement surrounding the move. There would be space for our huge family to stretch out some, so to speak. Thanks to multiple bedrooms in the floor plan, it allowed us the room to spread out. We wouldn't be right on top of each other. In addition to the multiple bedrooms, and bathrooms in each apartment, the complex offered screened-in breezeways, and lovely green space trees. There were coin-operated laundry rooms on the first floor of every building, along with mirrored-back, nicely-lit elevators that worked.

The playground areas, with swings and sandboxes, and the community center with picnic tables and areas designated for barbecuing were for tenants use only and were as nice as any. There were several basketball courts between buildings, fostering and sharing these amenities rivaled any the county had to offer. However, their location was in the best high-rent district St. Louis had to offer. In the P-I Government Projects, our rent was controlled according to income, and life was good. Our family was excited to live there and was very appreciative.

There had been several more additions to our ever-growing family. A week after my little brother Wilber's homecoming, the move-in magic had calmed down in our beautiful, sky-high dream house. I woke up, got dressed and went to kiss my new brother good morning before heading off to school, only to find him cold and lifeless in his crib. At only eleven days old, sadly, he was gone. There were now just twelve of us left and although we hadn't known Wilber long, we were still all very sad.

After several years, the Pruitt-Igoe Housing Projects we so loved, began to change. The exterior upkeep began to deteriorate, and the crime rate shot up. It became evident that enough data had not been factored into the long-range effects of stacking large numbers of people atop one another in close quarters. Sadly, the reality of that was beginning to show. Our father quickly jumped into action, organizing twenty-four of the most dedicated tenants and friends to patrol the complex in twelve-hour shifts. He and the "Igoe 24" wore white caps, white shirts and black pants, carried donated Louisville Slugger baseball bats, and used poor receptive walkie-talkies to communicate. Beginning a movement, the tenant-based security force that patrolled the grounds in the Pruitt-Igoe housing projects, gained worldwide notoriety. The "White Caps" held the line and stalled the government from writing off this community as a failed effort, allowing the projects to have several more years of good press. Holding down the fort by starting the first "neighborhood watch", afforded P-I to escape being tagged a failure for approximately twenty years. My dad's determination to be a problem solver, inspired me to follow in his footsteps.

It should be noted that it wasn't usually the residents who were causing the problems in P-I, it was people who came to P-I with the intent to cause trouble. They would come to push drugs, hide out, rob, and murder. Things happened there that make me sick to my stomach. It could've been something good. I believe if circumstances had been better, P-I could've been successful.

Meanwhile, our dad was getting a great deal of notoriety himself. Politicians, news publications, community newspapers, and community-based groups were coming to him at a furious pace, making him irresistible offers to reproduce the magic of the "White Caps" in their communities, thus birthing the tenant watch-group agencies as they are today. Dad was a busy man with meetings in various communities several evenings a week, and I was always right there with him at his side, in meetings before I knew the spelling of the word. Daddy's ability to bring people together and get them organized, spilled over into our involvement in politics. Me being daddy's baby girl, I would cry to follow him to meetings, birthing my interest in politics and then my love for it. I learned an ordinary person can make an extraordinary difference, which our dad did. For Dad, there would be no more going up to Chicago and driving a cab out of the airport on weekends for Uncle Eli's cabstand. He did other odd jobs as well and traveled to keep food on our table.

P-I was one of the worst designed projects in the country. Looking back now, it seems as if it was designed to fail. It puts me in the mind of Cabrini-Green in Chicago. You can't just stack people on top of each other, with little to no income, few jobs, and nothing constructive to do with themselves. They implode and self-destruct because of lack of educational and emotional stimulation. In my opinion, it's the equivalent of cutting someone's leg off and then criticizing them for being crippled.

We had moved from the Pruitt-Igoe Projects when the area changed, and it wasn't for the better, to Palm Street where the Lacey sisters had a four-family flat. Those several years were good; however, we desperately needed a home of our own, were the family could again spread out. Then, there came an offer our dad couldn't resist. Although I was already grown and married by this move, a home on DeGiverville Avenue became available with twelve rooms, a finished basement, and a fenced backyard where my parents could finally have a dog. Our mom had dreamed of an area once called Millionaire's Row, three blocks from Lindell Boulevard and four blocks from Forest Park. All that was needed was a yes and a small down payment; Momma immediately said yes. Our mom, a remarkable woman in her own right, was the fire that kept the family going. Though ill most of the time, she was remarkable, very virtuous. She poured all she knew into us, constantly teaching us how to treat others as we wished to be treated, not to pass judgment, and to give people the benefit of the doubt, until they prove otherwise. I took it all in and took it to heart. Mom said they would never have to move again and as always, Mom knew best. This became their forever family home.

Sadly, just two decades after being hailed for its glorious design and heraldry, Pruitt-Igoe's population had dwindled to just about sixteen buildings. The remaining buildings were boarded up. A decision was made to implode a couple buildings, which was shown on live TV. There were talks of renovation and rehabilitation for the remaining buildings, but those were scrapped and eventually, a decision was made to demolish the entire complex. Like others who lived there, I was sad to see it go; I had so many wonderful memories of growing up there. There's a reunion now, where people who used to live there get together and have a "family" reunion of sorts. It's a celebration, not of what was lost, but rather the everlasting memories and ties we have to each other.

Mom, Lubirtha Bolden and Dad, William S. Bolden Sr.

Chapter 2
LIFE AS A YOUNG WOMAN

My years as a young woman were spent looking at magazines like *Better Homes & Gardens* and imagining myself as the proper lady depicted in the magazine. Looking at those magazines exposed me to the kind of life I could have if I worked hard and was successful and trusted in our Lord and Savior, Jesus Christ. I trusted my mom's words and had the audacity to buy in. As that little girl, I had to take plenty before I could see making it as an option. I was bullied all through school, from kindergarten to middle school at Patrick Henry Grade School. It seemed when kids were bored with nothing to do, they picked on me.

Momma had a fancy friend named Ms. Cecil, whose children we watched while their party girl mom was on the road traveling as a backup singer. The summer before high school, Ms. Cecil bought and gifted me with my first wig and would bring me wigs whenever she toured, making my life more bearable and giving me a newfound confidence. That kind gesture, giving me a wig, opened up a whole new world for me. Ms. Cecil lived on our floor in Pruitt-Igoe and we would often all end up on the breezeway some evenings and it was always like a party.

I attended Vashon High School for two years at first. Then I transferred to Sumner High School to be with my best friend, Elaine Webb, who was dating and would later on marry my brother, Wardell. One of our classmates was Anna Mae Bullock, who the world now knows as the incomparable Tina Turner. Elaine and I graduated from Sumner in 1958.

During my high school summers, I worked at a community clinic, through a program funded by the government and staffed mostly with inner-city students attending high school, or college. They felt a job and a paycheck would hopefully contribute to their low-income family households, while learning a skill that could be parlayed into a career. My duties began as a main-entry corridor attendant for half a day, keeping the hallway free of trash and emptying the ashtrays and trashcans, mopping up spots and mishaps when needed.

The second half was spent with me directing people on how to get to hard-to-find offices in the annex; pediatrics, dental or prenatal care, or the social workers' growing suite of offices. During this time, I had a position as part of the social worker intake personnel. My duties included the ability to lower patient's bills if families could prove a hardship, and I knew how to answer to get them approved for the lowest co-pay, between two to twenty dollars. I often walked families back and made conversation along the way. People were used to me and had begun asking for me by name.

I was soon promoted to patient intake. I had even been tasked with the duty of streamlining the process for assistance. I loved my new position. Walking out front, I'd get my clients and bring them back, always offering them some juice or water I bought and kept in the cooler under my desk. After my third week en route to walk and greet a family, I fell hard on the wet floor. I used to say that floor should never be allowed to soak for days. Unfortunately, I slipped the disc in my lower back, practically shattering my dream of working to help others. I was out for a couple of months, undergoing painful rehab. It was then my mom and her sisters had me affirm daily, "If I could take it, I could make it." I affirmed it in my head and also in my heart.

The day finally came when I was ready to be released from my doctor's care. While at home, I had been given the job of making the registration process kinder and gentler, and the director was pleased with the changes I implemented. I was going back to a new position. The Kennedys were as beloved as Dr. King, both lost much too soon. Our late president, John F. Kennedy, had declared a war on poverty, developing the program that President Lyndon B. Johnson implemented after Kennedy's assassination. Several of my suggestions had been included. There was about a two-year cloud of darkness over our nation, as some people said and others believed, President Johnson did more than President Kennedy ever could have. We had been a nation in transition, mourning a beloved son, and a country transitioning into a promising future. I found my niche, and I went to work daily doing what I loved, helping everyday people. That was and still is my passion.

After graduating from Sumner in 1958, I attended Harris-Stowe State University, received a certificate in business from Hubbard's Business College and a certificate in management from Washington University. In fact, I garnered several certificates, going to Harris Teachers College in the evenings. I started out working at the Human Development Corporation and later became a branch manager. I worked there, helping people. There, we gave out butter and cheese, the commodities for everything. We provided social service, helping people with their utilities, providing much-needed services. It kept the young people off the streets, helped them to keep the community clean, and at the same time, we taught them how to be productive citizens. They'd tell me when they saw me at the Pruitt-Igoe reunions, "Mrs. Thompson, you got me my first job."

Working with people daily and finally enjoying a social life, my wigs afforded me the boost in confidence and self-esteem I needed. I had a close circle of lifelong friends and

I had a routine. Two weekends out of the month, we would go roller-skating. On the alternating weekends, we would go to rent parties, which were house parties put on to raise money for families to keep from being evicted. These parties were the bomb back then. Chicken wings, hot dogs, or hamburgers off the grill were sold, along with ice-cold sodas. No hard liquor was sold though.

It was at a rent party where I first noticed this tall, caramel-colored guy from Martin, Tennessee, turning up at the same places we frequented. His name was Jack Thompson and my best friend, Elaine, promised me his interest was in me, not her. I didn't believe her at first, because he could have his pick of any other woman there. Besides, Elaine was beautiful, with a head of hair; her crowning glory, hanging to her waist. Then, our eyes met; he looked at me with such intensity, I had to look away as I was still fairly shy. He gave me goosebumps.

One Friday evening, the basement was packed. As usual, Jack Thompson had a comfortable spot, where he could see us all. It had been several weeks now, and Elaine was right. Jack walked up to me getting all in my personal space, asking, "Betty Bolden, would you like to dance?"

This was the first dance of three in a row. The DJ usually slowed down the pace, playing the slow jams at this time. So, on this the first of many dances, I conjured up the nerve and allowed him to lead me to the center of the dance floor, where we danced under strobe lights that created a cozy atmosphere. I was enjoying the smell of his cologne, fully content and snug in his strong arms, in the middle of the dance floor, yet feeling like it was just the two of us by ourselves.

My elation would soon be short-lived, however. I guess to some like Jackie Bardot, she felt she should've been in his arms instead of me. After a while, I thought I felt a firm tug from behind, followed by an undeniable vicious and hard tug, leaving my wig on the floor. Covering my eyes and screaming a deeply wounded scream that seemed to come from the depths of my soul, I was led to the bathroom by Elaine. I was embarrassed, hurt, and feeling humiliated.

After picking up my wig, Jack came and stood outside the door. He gave Elaine my hair and told her, "Elaine, I'll be right here and I promise I'll accompany her home, no matter how long it takes for her to calm down. Please let her know I'm here for her."

Elaine helped me pull myself together, even though I swore I couldn't face anyone, especially not Jack Thompson. "I'd rather be swallowed up under the bathroom floor than to face him ever again in life."

After roughly two hours, Elaine told me the party had ended a whole hour earlier than usual, but Jack was still there. She said, "He ain't leaving."

When she finally convinced me to come out, I wouldn't release her hand, so she and I faced Jack together. He blocked my path and the next words from his mouth soothed my wounded soul like a balm to my aching heart. Jack got down on bended knee and said, "I'm so sorry that was done to you. I want to be a part of your life, Betty Lou Bolden. I want to protect you, so no one or nothing ever hurts you like that ever again. The world is cruel and I want to be your soldier guy, protecting and shielding you from tonight's kinda hurt, harm, or danger. And if you agree and your dad is in agreement, I want to make you my wife in due time."

Jack was speaking truth to the feelings he said he had for me. I thanked God for the man he sent me, because his actions that evening endeared him to the family instantly.

Best friend in High school, Elaine Webb-Bolden

CHAPTER 3
WIFE…MOTHER…FAMILY

From that night on we were inseparable, and after a years engagement, we were wed. Married life was quite the adjustment, full of ups and downs. During those early years Dorie, one of my younger brothers, married Dolores Davis, Miles Davis' niece. Sadly, five years after his marriage, my brother was killed by an unknown assailant. He was twenty-one years old at the time with no children and worked at General Motors. Tragedy had been an unwelcomed visitor to my family's doorstep once again.

I'm not saying it's been all crystal stairs, I'm saying we rose above the drama of married life whenever it rose its ugly head, by always climbing and reaching for that top-shelf devotion that God is. We worked things out by going back to our core principles of the early years. It's been fifty-eight years and four children later, and we can truly smile when we look back over the job we did as parents. We were always active in the community and raised our children to do the same.

I thank God daily for my husband, Jack, and his being devoted to our family and always encouraging me in my efforts and the children in theirs. Jack is the head of our family, God-fearing, the engine that truly drives the Thompson family machine and the love of my life. He hails from Martin, Tennessee, a small town about twelve miles from the Kentucky state line. Jack told me that in 1950, the population in his hometown was almost 3100 people. He used to work grinding up corn to feed calves to earn money and also worked at the local movie theater, cleaning up and punching tickets, in order to earn the chance to watch a movie. He said, "I used to mow our landlord's yard. We weren't allowed to enter through the front door; we had to go around to the back. Sometimes, the lady of the house would bring us some lemonade to the back door, sit it down and run back in the house, like she was scared our black was going to rub off." There were very few inside jobs for black people; any jobs available to them were almost always outside, the indoor jobs being reserved for white people. Jack left Martin as soon as he was able, joining the Air Force in order to be afforded better opportunities.

After Jack's distinguished Air Force military service as a Military Police Officer, otherwise known as an MP, he worked in several major corporate security agencies. His last and longest was with General Motors, where he was chief of the security team for the bullet plant. He later retired, yet never stopped working either. Jack worked with our oldest son, Tony, several times throughout his retirement, tweaking the security protocols for the building group as needed. He believes one had to lead as an example for the family to seek that example in their own lives. Jack drives back to Martin every year for homecoming, which gives him a chance to reconnect with family and friends who also left in search of better employment opportunities.

Our eldest child, Anthony "Tony" Thompson, is founder and CEO of KWAME Building Group, a construction management company. Tony is a proud member of Kappa Alpha Psi Fraternity. He believes in giving back, so he provides young, fresh out of college professionals, with jobs. Giving them a chance to do right and make a living for their families. Tony also has a foundation, which endows educational scholarships, with a yearly celebrity golf tournament. Having given away over a million dollars since its inception, which is quite a special accomplishment, Tony built a music studio that has artists who co-own all their music endeavors. Tony established the Gentleman's Club, which is a mentoring program for young men. Our second son, Tyrone, worked diligently alongside him with the club. Tony encourages his staff to be involved in the club, teaching these young men how to be gentlemen. The group also sponsors other types of educational programs throughout several other school systems in St. Louis. Tony also uses his production studio to surprise people, helping to make their dreams come true. These youth and young adults from at-risk circumstances are deserving. He is a devoted husband and father, to wife, Kim, and children, Kristin and Michael.

Tyrone Thompson was a police officer, rising to the rank of police chief later on in his career. Tyrone was the past president of the Dr. MLK Nonviolent St. Louis Support Group, where the "Kingian" non-violent principles were taught. Ironically, Tyrone would become a victim of gun violence himself, the victim of a botched armed robbery. He was an investigator for the Attorney General's office in

St. Louis, an active parent with the Hazelwood PTO, a super great dad, and Tony's chief cyber security officer at KWAME Building Group, and Tony's right-hand man. He departed this life, June 5, 2010. Tyrone was the father of three wonderful children: daughter Kayla and sons, Tyler and Tyrell. Unfortunately, Tyrell would die in 2016, from eerily similar circumstances to those of his dad's; an attempted armed robbery gone wrong.

My only daughter, Sonja M. Thompson-Branscomb, is a document specialist for the drafting and engineering department at KWAME. Sonja, a high-end club owner/investor, is putting the finishing touches on plans and designs for a groundbreaking, transitional-living housing facility, where women and children will spend up to two years, rebuilding their broken lives. The self-contained program will have a mandatory curriculum on site for moms and children working toward self-sufficiency and independence, which includes classes on money management. The positions will be rotating residents to volunteer one day a month, either in the kitchen and/or a day in the day care, as part of their being there. The goal is to have the women emerge qualified to have more opportunities despite their circumstances; better not bitter is the goal. Sonja spends one month a year collecting blankets, gloves, socks, hats and scarves, along with anything else the homeless may need. Then, she and a crew of her friends distribute them the first cold day of the winter. She has done this for several years now without fanfare or publicity. This apple didn't fall far from her mama Betty's tree, helping others is indeed a family affair. Every year, she takes two to three busloads of students to HBCU campuses for college tours. Sonja has two lovely daughters, Ayanna and Imani. She is also known as the karaoke queen.

Last, but not least is Kwame, the baby boy of the clan. Kwame is a successful lawyer and owner of a prestigious Atlanta law firm, licensed to practice law in Missouri and Georgia. Personal injury is one of his most sought-after services. Kwame is a professor and an administrative judge for the City of Atlanta. He is dedicated to maintaining legal counsel for Tony's company, as well as an investor in club ownership with his sister, Sonja. Kwame is an aspiring bodybuilder. He is a fraternity brother, a member of Kappa Alpha Psi along with his brother, Tony, as well as a very charitable attorney who always finds time working pro-bono cases helping people who can't afford an attorney. The list of charities he works with is expansive. He has run for public office in the past. Kwame has aspirations of a life in public service, just like his mom. To date, Kwame remains single and loves it.

MY HEROES

Grandchildren: (top row) Kristin, Tyrell (deceased), Tyler, Michael (bottom row) Kayla, Ayanna, Imani

Sisters: Sandra Ella Bolden Stittum, Self, Rosemary Bolden Banner (deceased)

Nikki Whitmore Lloyd, Tyrone Thompson (deceased), Stephen Piphus, unknown, Self, Former Mayor of Pagedale, MO Mary Carter, Faustenia Morrow, April Hendrix Brown, and Rosalyn Smith.
Fundraiser for Betty Thompson for State Representative.

Jack, Tony, Tyrone, Lewis Branscomb (son-in-law), Kwame Thompson.
Sonja's Wedding

Daughter, Sonja

Son and Grandson, Tyrone and Tyrell Thompson

Daughter-in-law, Kim Thompson

Daughter-in-law, Victoria Thompson

CHAPTER 4
FINDING MY PURPOSE AND PASSION

I worked diligently to be of service to others my entire life. My first job was at the L.H.I. health clinic, taking the job to help my parents out before I went to work at the Human Development Corporation. My dream was always to go back to help solve some of the problems I grew up with. If we have a desire and ability to help those trapped in poverty to get out, we can do it with determination. I've worked for the St. Louis Board of Elections and the St. Louis Marriage License Bureau. Wherever there was a need, I was sure to be there. My greatest glory though, was working at HDC. That's when I was truly in my element, helping others, solving problems, showing people that their circumstances didn't make them any less human. I feel that it not only empowered me to help them, and that power spilled over and I was able to pour it into my fellow man. I kept it in mind that I could inspire other women to know that they too, could make it, if they kept on trying, forged ahead and kept on pushing.

Just as my mother instilled in me a "put your shoulder to the wall and push" attitude, I tried to pass that down to my clients and my children. I was never afraid of hard work, and didn't understand the meaning of no.

CHAPTER 5
RUNNING FOR OFFICE

In December 1973, tragedy introduced itself to my family again. We were on our way to a General Motors Christmas party. I believe God always gives us warning signs, if we pay attention and adhere to them. He gave us three different warnings on this night. The first warning was that we didn't feel like going, and we were always very outgoing. We were running very late, which was a rather rare occurrence for us. Jack stopped by my mother's house and when he told her he had a very bad headache, she gave him a Valium. By the time he got home, I had been waiting for so long, I didn't even want to go. We drove about six blocks from the house when the car sputtered and we ran out of gas, our second sign. This was yet another unusual occurrence, because we never ran out of gas.

Jack wound up walking up the block to the nearest gas station and came back with a gas can full of enough gas to get us to the station for a fill-up. After gassing up, we headed to the hotel where the party was being held, only to discover we were at the wrong hotel, which I found odd because we never got lost. I believe that was the third sign. It took us about a half-hour to find the correct hotel.

There was plenty of food and drinks and Jack had one or two drinks and ate something. I didn't know he'd taken a Valium. In fact, he seemed perfectly fine to me. We proceeded to leave the party after a while and he got in the car, then pulled around for me to get in. When I got in, I said to him, "Let me drive."

"No, I'm going to drive."

"If I can't drive, I'm not going to ride," I told him, as I got out and stood in front of the hotel. He pulled off laughing and I laughed too, figuring he'd turn right around and come back for me. Soon, one of his coworkers, Larry Davis, came out with his wife Dolores, and they asked me why I was standing there.

I explained what happened to them, adding, "I thought Jack was coming back." So, they kindly offered me a ride home. After they dropped me off, the phone was ringing as I was going in the house. When I answered, it was St. John's Mercy Hospital on the other end, telling me I needed to get there right away. "Mrs. Thompson, we need you to get here as fast as you can. Your husband, Jack, has been in a serious accident."

I called my parents and they came to take me to St. John's. When we got there and inquired about Jack's condition, the doctor informed me, "There is a broken-up body back there. His neck is broken, along with his arm and leg. Jack's broken the seventh vertebrae. In all honesty, we don't know if he's going to make it."

Jack didn't know that I spent the night at the hospital and the next morning, I went to get Tony and Tyrone to see their dad. When we got back to the hospital, I let the boys walk into the room ahead of me. Jack burst into tears, just as the kids started crying too. Jack kept telling me, "I don't know what to say to you." Later on, Jack said he didn't realize that I'd gotten back out of the car before he pulled off and when the boys walked in the room, Jack immediately thought that I'd been killed in the accident.

We soon found out that Jack had to be put in traction for months, completely immobile. When it was time to start physical therapy, he endured a lot of intense pain and suffering, learning how to walk again. The accident had crushed his ankle and he had surgery to put pins in to keep the ankle intact. During this time, I was working in Kinloch. Every day, I'd catch the bus to work, and then afterwards, catch the bus home to prepare his meal. Then, I'd head back off to work, before doing it again.

Soon, the doctors recommended he try swimming as a part of his therapy, citing how studies had shown that swimming is easier on the joints and muscles.

We'd need to build a pool in order for him to swim. To build a swimming pool, we'd need a permit from city council. Visiting our city council would soon prove to be daunting. "I'm here to apply for a permit to build a swimming pool on my property," I told them.

After a rousing round of boisterous laughter, followed by looks of stern resistance, they gave me a ludicrous answer. "Mrs. Thompson, no black person who's ever lived on the north side of University City can possibly afford to build a swimming pool." That incident not only angered me, it sparked a burning desire within me to run for city council, just so I could change that.

Once he was able to, Jack began driving again, not letting that accident deter him from going anywhere he wanted to go. He immediately drove down to Martin, Tennessee, to visit his family and for homecoming and continued to do so for many years. "The accident gave me a new appreciation for life," he told me.

I've always felt that God had a plan for our lives, because Jack not only survived that accident, he walked again, something the doctors were skeptical about. Looking back at the accident, I realized that I was supposed to be in the car with Jack at that time. Had I been in the car riding alongside him, I would have been killed. The passenger side where I would've been sitting was crushed. The hood was sticking up and would have gone straight through me.

***

Jack was now feeling better and able to get around, albeit with lingering pain, but something was still bothering me. I kept hearing the derisive words of the city council, echoing repeatedly in the back of my mind. *"Mrs. Thompson, no black person who's ever lived on the north side of University City can possibly afford to build a swimming pool."*

Being a woman of action and a "get it done" mindset, along with all the experience I'd garnered watching my father in politics, I knew what it was going to take. I immediately began campaigning. My son, Kwame and a young lady named Faustenia Morrow, organized a group of young people called YOPAC, which stands for Young Organized Political Action Committee. The group consisted of April Hendrix Brown, Jonathan LaGrone, Rosalyn Smith, Nikki Whitmore Lloyd, Stephen Piphus, Kim Royal Thompson and Marlon Wharton. YOPAC sprang into action by utilizing a grassroots approach, such as door knocking, phone calls, pamphlets, and flyers. I ran my campaign without any fundraising and held a ten-block parade in University City. Having the parade helped me to win the 1980 election against a white engineer. After I won the election for state representative in 1997, YOPAC disbanded and they all moved on to other successful endeavors.

Alopecia Bill signed by former Governor of Missouri, Bob Holden

Being the first African-American female to be on University City's City Council only proved to me how behind we were as African Americans and how fast we had to run to catch up. I served on the board for eighteen years. I wish Momma could have been there to see me run for office and win, but sadly, we'd lost her in 1978, followed by Daddy eighteen years later.

I've often seen other African-Americans treated unfairly. Back when I heard Dr. Martin Luther King, Jr. speak at a local church, I'd started organizing marches, pickets and sit-ins in my hometown. I knew Dr. King spoke the truth and things needed to change for us. During that time, I met and maintained a close friendship with Coretta Scott King that continued long after his passing. I took a keen interest in civil rights and the rights of others. I marched, picketed and protested for justice and freedom, not just for us, but for all people because I believed that everybody deserved to have the same rights. I felt people should be judged on their actions, not the color of their skin. I also realized that he made a huge sacrifice, giving his time and ultimately, his life, for what he believed in. If that's not love for your fellow man, I don't know what is. I am past President and one of the organizers of the Dr. Martin Luther King Jr. Support Group here in St. Louis. Reverend Sterling Lands, one of my first campaign managers when I ran for city council and police captain, Charles Alphin, were also organizers. Captain Alphin, who now lives in Atlanta, is involved with The King Center. For years, we'd charter buses every year, headed to his celebration. We currently have a student awareness program, designed to teach them about his non-violent philosophies and principles and instructing them on ways to solve things in a non-violent fashion. I've realized that all black people are not good, and all white people are not bad. It takes all of us working together to make this world a better place.

With Coretta Scott King

The Urban League of Metropolitan St. Louis, under the direction of Bill Doggett, was awarded the anti-poverty program. The anti-poverty program was instituted by President Johnson in 1964, declaring a war on poverty. A couple years later, the program was turned over to the Human Development Corporation. I worked with this program for twenty-six years and it's still in existence today. That is my most wonderful memory, because I was able to be right there with those who were struggling, less fortunate, and it gave me not only a chance to help them, it made me realize how blessed I was and grateful for what I had. It consistently put things into the proper perspective for me.

During the course of my tenure in public office, there were several instances that occurred where I believe I was put in the right place at the right time to be of service, answering the calling from a higher power.

One such occurrence was when a young lady raising three kids on her own, called me saying she was about to commit suicide. She lived near Pruitt-Igoe and had to build a makeshift fire in her house because she no heat, no lights and no water. Her situation was critical, and she was desolate, because her man had left her and the children to be with another woman. After speaking with her for a while, I invited her to come and hear me speak to a group of women at Grace Hill House.

I didn't know if she'd come or not, but right after the speech, she let me know that she'd heard what I said. I spoke with her again. "He's gone on, he's happy, he's moved on. Would it be fair to your children for you to check out because he moved on? You tried to do the best you could on your own by yourself, now why don't you give life a try? Won't you give God a try? All black people aren't good and all white people aren't bad, there's good in everybody." I tried my best to speak life into this young woman, to let her know that although her situation seemed hopeless, there was always a way.

She hugged me and assured me she would give things another try. Four months later, she reached out to me again. By trusting in what I told her, and understanding that everyone wasn't bad or good, just based on the color of their skin, she got help. She was able to get welfare and a part-time job and was doing as well as can be expected.

Another instance was when I organized a group of hard-core young men, some were on drugs and some were gang members. They were unemployed young people who lost their way. One of the things I did to help was to bus them every week to General Motors, Anheuser-Busch, and McDonnell-Douglas to apply for jobs. Most of them were hired at the ammunition plant. I estimate that I managed to secure about two hundred jobs from 1960 to 1965. In addition, I secured jobs for residents who were head of their households and for eligible teenagers who were old enough to work.

The young men offered to pay me and I refused, explaining to them, "That was my job, it's what I was supposed to do." I wanted to make absolutely sure that no one could ever say they "bought" their jobs.

I'm often stopped in the street by men and women who say, "You got me my first job. Thank you." The first African American mayor of St. Louis, Freeman Bosley, Jr. told me that I even got him his first job, along with acting Sheriff of St. Louis, Steve "Steve-Bo" Chalmers. Former heavyweight champions, Michael and Leon Spinks, credit me with helping them secure their very first jobs.

The Bible says, "Can anything good come out of Nazareth?" I've often said, "Can anything good come out of Pruitt-Igoe?" One of my proudest achievements and living proof that yes, good did come out of Pruitt-Igoe, is the Willie and Ruby Stevens family, who had twelve children growing up in Pruitt-Igoe. Ruby is my maternal first cousin. I was able to get the children summer jobs, and Willie got a job at McDonnell-Douglas, where he worked until he retired. All twelve of the Stevens children are professionals. Two are doctors, one works in law enforcement, a couple are business consultants; in fact, one daughter started an abused women's program and one of the sisters works there as an administrator, two work in the medical field, one's a project manager, two work in education and one's a certified plumber.

Ruby and Willie Stevens

Ruby and Willie's Sons

Ruby and Willie's Daughters

This goes to show that if we invest a little time, energy, love and understanding in people, we can encourage them to rise above their adversity and achieve reachable goals.

As in every job, there are highs and then there are lows. One young man had a confrontation with another and pulled out a gun, intending to shoot the other. I was able to convince "Red Dog" to give me the gun. I had a serious conversation with them, explaining to them, "Y'all are friends; this is not what you want to do." They made up, shook hands and went their separate ways.

Another time during one neighborhood board meeting, a hard-core young man signed in and left. A few minutes later, we heard shots and right after that, he returned and sat down in the meeting like nothing had happened. Later on, though, he was found dead.

I had a coworker, Barbara Petty, gunned down on the way to her car to pick me up. We were supposed to be going to the funeral for Chairman Larry Johnson's father. Chairman Johnson, at the time, was Chairman of the Board for HDC. As I waited for her, I received a call that she'd been shot. To this day, sadly, her murder remains unsolved. I think about her often. She was a good employee; honest, dedicated and loyal.

I've had contracts placed on my life, when I was branch manager for Pruitt-Igoe Gateway Center, the anti-poverty program, as well as tenant manager of the housing project with close friend, Ruby Russell. Apparently, someone felt that we, along with Congressman William "Bill" Clay, Sr., were informants for the police, telling them where they stored and sold their drugs, which was untrue. We knew nothing of the sort and couldn't inform the police of these actions.

Sometimes when you cheer for people, care for them and keep consideration for them in mind, some will take your kindness for weakness. That has actually happened to me as well. I once hired a secretary from Jefferson City, while I was working in the Jefferson City State House. She was a very kind young lady involved with a guy who was locked up in the Jefferson City County Jail. He kept calling her at work, asking her to make three-way calls for him and to lay the phone down. Unbeknownst to her, he was making drug deals over the phone.

A few months later, the feds called my house, letting me hear recordings of the young man conducting deals on the phone. I immediately had to let the young lady go, even though she reassured me that she knew nothing about his dealings.

I've always tried to help young people and to be a good example for them. However, even the best intentions can go sadly astray. I had a teenage girl approach me who was seeking employment. Senator Bland and I shared an apartment in Jefferson City and her parents asked if the young teen could stay with us. We said yes and she moved in. Senator Rita Heard Days, and my secretary, Nikki Whitmore Lloyd lived in the apartment below us.

The police knocked on our door one night, looking for the young lady's boyfriend. We didn't know he was in town at the time. The officers asked, "Did someone come in here?"

"No," we replied.

"Ma'am, do y'all mind if we search the premises?"

Having nothing to hide, we quickly said, "Sure."

During the search, the police discovered that although the young lady denied it, she'd hidden the guy under my bed. The police swiftly arrested him and took him to jail. We went to the jail and found out he'd stolen a car in St. Louis, to come see the girl and find a job. We knew absolutely nothing about this young man. Finally, at about two o'clock in the morning, she confessed that she knew who he was. Unfortunately, I had to send her back to her parents in St. Louis.

What did I learn from these experiences? "Sometimes a bought lesson, is a taught lesson." All through these experiences, I never lost my faith or the desire to help people or to find the good in them. Many would say I was crazy to continue to help, even after these incidents, but stopping never crossed my mind. What if I'd stopped? The very next person that needed my help, that would've been successful because I didn't give up on them, might not have made it if I didn't help.

Keep in mind that two of my brothers, along with my two sisters and I had alopecia, and we didn't know the name of what it was that caused us to have no hair. I might not have known what it was called, but I could recall everything that was said to me or about me because of it. In fact, I didn't learn the name of the condition until I went to Jefferson City, Missouri, as a legislator in 2000, and that was only because I met a white woman who was devastated by her four-and-a-half-year-old daughter's lack of hair. Upon talking to her, I found out the little girl was about to go to school and didn't have any hair on her head, and her mother didn't know what to do about it and was distraught. That's when she told me that her daughter suffered from alopecia.

Alopecia? I thought. A lack of hair? That's what we have. When I finally found out that there was an actual name for our condition and lack of hair, I spoke to a doctor and looked it up. From what was explained to me, alopecia is a common autoimmune disease that results in the loss of hair on the scalp and elsewhere. Males and females of all ages and races can suffer from it, and it most often occurs in childhood, as it did with my siblings and me. What happens is the hair follicles are mistakenly attacked by your own immune system, resulting in the hair growth stage slowing down or in some cases, stopping completely, because something triggers the immune system to suppress the hair follicle. They still don't know what this trigger is, and where it comes from. They believe it to possibly be hereditary, but there isn't absolute scientific information that actively supports that data. Scientists believe that it's polygenic, (containing many genes), from both parents, along with environmental contributions.

It was all so confusing to me, but at least now I knew what it was called. I also knew what that little girl was going through, because I'd been in her shoes, so to speak. I didn't want any more children to go through that, or any parents to have to feel that sense of loss and despair because they can't help their child. It fueled a desire in me to get legislature passed to ensure that insurance would pay for "medically necessary" hairpieces for children.

I've sponsored quite a few bills, but one of the ones that was close to my heart was the Alopecia Bill, passed in 2003. It was designed for youths, ages zero to eighteen who need hair prosthesis. To sum it up neatly, it dealt with permanent hair loss and basically stated that insurance companies would have to pay for it. This was truly one of my greatest achievements and one that I'm still proud of to this day.

Another bill I helped sponsor was for police legislation. Tyrone actually helped me to write this one. Essentially, the bill would require that a police officer's record follow them to a new jurisdiction, if they changed jobs. When people fill out an application for a job, they check your past work history at other jobs, or your personnel record if you transfer to a different position within the same company. Previously, if police officers went to another jurisdiction, it was like they were starting off with a clean slate. If there was something that was a cause for concern on their personnel record, no one at the new precinct would know about it. Sadly, this bill didn't pass; they amended and repackaged this bill to the point where it wasn't recognizable as the original bill we'd written. It is still my true belief that if this bill had passed, Michael Brown, from Ferguson, Missouri, would possibly still be alive today. The officer that shot him had been terminated from one jurisdiction after another for various reasons, only to be hired in others without fear of any consequences or repercussions.

There's also the wrongful imprisonment bill, which would provide restitution for someone wrongfully imprisoned. I knew a young lady, Ellen Reasonover, who went to prison from our community at twenty-four years old. She called the police to report information that she thought would help them catch the murderers of a gas station attendant. She soon found herself charged with the man's murder, then tried and convicted. One juror refused to vote for her execution, so she was sentenced to fifty years in prison without the possibility of parole. Had there been a unanimous vote, Ellen would've received the death penalty. After serving sixteen of those fifty years, a federal judge threw out her conviction, saying it was "fundamentally unfair" and ordered her immediate release. Several things led to his fundamentally unfair ruling. There were no active witnesses to the crime, no physical evidence, no link to the murder weapon. The money in the register was still intact, and there was money still sitting in the unlocked safe. There were also audiotapes withheld that disputed the prosecution's witnesses, and evidence that the prosecution had paid one of the witnesses, along with dropping charges for another's testimony.

They released her, but she'd lost sixteen years. Can you imagine sixteen whole years of your life just rubbed away like nothing? At the time of her imprisonment, Ellen left behind a two-year-old daughter, who was grown when she was released. My state didn't provide any type of restitution at the time. So, she came home to no job, no chance, just nothing. Unfortunately, this bill didn't pass either so to this day; Missouri doesn't provide restitution for wrongfully convicted persons.

Yet another bill I stood firmly behind was the anti-cross burning bill. I consider it a hate crime for people to burn a cross in someone else's yard. In fact, I feel that we need stronger laws on all types of hate crimes, clear and concise, so there's no confusion. We need stiffer penalties, not just smacks on the wrist for obvious and deliberate hate crime acts.

We've come a long way, both legally and morally, but there's still work to be done. Now isn't the time to become complacent and relaxed, not when civil rights are still being unequally treated to justice in courts, not when people are still being profiled by law enforcement, not when the quality of education suffers greatly because of an unbalanced footing. As Dr. King used to say, "The time is always ripe to do right." This means, anytime is a good time to step out, step up, and speak out. We still have bigotry, racism, separatism; it's not always out in the open, but it's there. Every time we let an instance "slide", we're giving the perpetrator permission to do it again, by showing them that we won't do anything about it. Being complacent gives a notion that we're the equivalent of doormats. We must get up, stand up, speak up, and show that we're stronger than that and remember that it's an ongoing process. We can't win the fight and then sit down; instead, we must be forever vigilant, always on the lookout.

Additionally, another issue near and dear to my heart is the educational systems. The system is sorely lacking in materials, safety, caring and concern. The wheel is broken and needs fixing. Teachers need to have what they need in order to teach, their credentials need to be current and up-to-date. Students need to know that someone truly cares about them learning. Parents need to start parenting, keeping the lines of communication open with teachers and their children, making sure the kids do their homework and study for tests. Lawmakers need to ensure that laws and funding are in place to take care of the school systems financially, and taxpayers need to hold the lawmakers accountable. All these groups need to work together as a cohesive unit, supporting each other. This will help to better our school systems for the generations coming up. Although I wasn't on any educational committees, I made sure to support those who were on the committees and on the floor as well.

I literally stopped traffic in St. Louis when I found out minority participation on construction for our highways were low. We organized protests, putting people out to stop traffic's progress so they would hire more minorities. We wanted to call attention to it, and we achieved that goal.

We passed legislation on bills that will help to prevent racial profiling in Missouri and other places, as well as creating a Woman's Offender Program, which would give emotional and other types of aid and support to women coming out of prison.

Among my list of achievements, just to name a few:

- Voted President of Women in Municipal Government in Los Angeles, (1981).

- First African American elected to Women in Government – an arm of the prestigious National League of Cities, representing all fifty states (1987).

- First African American female arrested in Washington, DC, for protesting Apartheid in South Africa (1988).

- First African American female to serve on the cabinet of St. Louis County Executive Democrat George "Buzz" Westfall (1991).

- Served as Democratic Majority Whip while representing part of St. Louis County (District 72) in the Missouri House of Representatives (2000).

- First Democrat to be elected by the Republican Majority as Vice-chair of the Ethics Committee (2002).

- April 15, 2004 was declared Betty L. Thompson Day by the Missouri House of Representatives.

- Received the 2006 MLK Spirit Award from the University City School Board and City Council.

- Received the Gwen B. Giles Award.

- *St. Louis Post-Dispatch* Outstanding Women in Leadership.

- Ernest and DeVerne Lee Calloway Award.

- KMOX Radio and Suburban Journal's Women of Achievement Award.

- Received the Drum Major for Peace Award by the St. Louis Cleary Coalition.

- Received Outstanding Legislative Mother of the Year Award from U.S. State Senator, Jet Banks. (Senate's Mother of the Year).

- Received the Rosa Parks Award for Lifetime Achievement for a long career in public service, given by the St. Louis County NAACP.

- Hosted a radio program on KATZ and KIRL for over twenty-five years. According to Bernie Hayes, who is an outstanding TV and radio personality, I was the first African American to have a talk show on the radio.

- Received the Michael Brown Justice Award.

- Received the Mound City Bar Association Award.

- Entered into Sumner High School's Hall of Fame.

- Entered into Sigma Gamma Rho's Hall of Fame at Harris State College as a full member.

- *The Riverfront Times* listed me as Best of St. Louis – Politician of the Year.

- Letters from several sitting presidents, including Presidents Reagan and Clinton.

Better Family Life, a non-profit in St. Louis, works to help build and maintain strong families. They honored me with a portrait in their project, "Beyond the Walls". The project, which began in 2011, was designed to beautify vacant buildings along Page Boulevard between Union and Kings Highway. Instead of seeing plain boards when they pass by, people see artists' renditions of prominent African Americans. The paintings are done by two local artists; Chris Green, who honors successful African Americans with St. Louis connections, and Cornell McKay, who paints symbolic African Americans. Tyrone has a portrait there as well.

One of the absolute highlights of my career was when President Obama, who was not yet the president at the time, walked past Tony and me, and said, "Hi, Mom." It makes me smile with pride every time I think of it.

CHAPTER 6

HOW I DEAL WITH LIFE, THE UPS AND DOWNS

Life has been full of tragedy, sprinkled with disappointment and trials. I lost my Big Mama at a young age, and I feel Momma left us much too soon. Even though Daddy lived a long life up to the age of eighty-three, I feel he left me too soon as well. Two of my younger brothers were killed, and I lost two of my older brothers to brain cancer. My older brothers always protected me, throughout my life, and they both grew up to be golden glove boxers. People always ask me how I deal with everyday struggles, life, and trials and tribulations. To be honest, I remember Daddy always being a man of action, solving problems instead of lamenting them. Also, I always refer back to the mantra Momma taught me many years ago. "If you can take it, you can make it." How do I deal with whatever life throws at me? I believe fervently in the power of prayer. I also believe in immersing myself in being a good servant of God. Helping people has always been my calling, my passion and my life's blood. I wake up every day with the thought of how I can help someone else, always striving to be active in my community and to help others. One of the reasons I feel I was so successful, is because I've always had a very supportive family. Another reason, without a doubt, is my faith and conviction in God and a strong determination.

Oftentimes, life circumstances dictate our mission and with that, God chooses who he uses. *A woman I grew to be, a child of God I'm privileged to be. A good wife and mother I came to be, a virtuous woman I chose to be, and black I must be.* With all these "be's" in place, I count everything as a blessing from above. I feel that I was destined to help others because of where I came from. We didn't have much, but we had love and a burning desire to make it through. I grew up in an atmosphere of giving, loving, and genuine care for each other, and that spread out into wanting to do more to help.

I was and still am always willing to assist others in any way I can, mainly because I know whatever the conflict, it could have been my family or I that was in need. And the truth is, no matter how self-made we think we are, no one gets to their destination without the help of others. We were always taught that we are all God's own. I've never thought or felt that I was better than anyone else, nor did I ever feel inferior to anyone else. Momma used to say, "You are your most important person, so never allow anyone to make you feel anything different." I took that to heart and implemented that in everything I said or did.

I'd like to dedicate this to every female; any creed, race, color or age. If you've ever thought about giving up, throwing in the towel, or simply walking away, STOP! Hold up; hold on a little while longer. Change is the only constant thing in life and it will always come to pass. I was taught early on that if one has the patience, sprinkled with a little bit of faith, things will shift, most likely for the better. We can bring a permanent solution to a temporary problem, but we have to be willing to move our feet.

After all my years of public service, I still get excited as ever about new projects and the people in the trenches, where the real work begins. I've always been more comfortable working with the grassroots folk, that's when

I'm in my element. I have no problems with the scholars and elitists; I just prefer not to have to be saddled with them. I'll take my everyday people every time when rolling up the sleeves to do some real work. I'm winding down a bit nowadays; however, my most rewarding work looking back, was when I was a young girl maintaining the corridor hall of the clinic, meeting and helping all kinds of people. Then, there was the Human Development Corporation Anti-Poverty Program, which took me from worker to center director of several programs. There were stints working with the NAACP I enjoyed. Being the Dr. King Group President of St. Louis, and running the Tyrone Thompson Institute for Nonviolence (since his passing), the KWAME Foundation president and many more, simply to name a few.

I went from the project house, to the county house, to the state house, proof that where you grow up and your circumstances don't define who you're destined to be. I've been in the house of women in municipal government, to the Dr. King's Drum Major for Peace Place.

I stress my words to all; however, my message is for women in particular, because as women, we hold up the world. So, when the hiccups of life come along, and they will come, know that tough times aren't long lasting, but tough people are. I'm living proof that in trying times, if you can take it, you, too, can make it. Believe it, receive it, and make it your own. And women, trust you've been tested and it's true; if we can birth the baby into this world, we can guide them through it. Know that your life has a meaning and a purpose. If you can't discern it, seek it anew daily in meditation with your higher power. Know also that you all are somebody; you are God's child. If you want him to use you, keep your heart free from hate, keep your mouth from spreading gossip, and keep the temple (body) free of impurities. I modeled myself after my mother. Momma didn't smoke, drink, cuss or hang out. She was a virtuous woman, and I embodied and embraced that. Fill your life with love and happiness, spread sunshine and scatter it about. Remember daily to get up, sit up, dress up, pray up, pay up, vote up and never throw your hands up in despair.

I was blinded for ten years; my vision was gone. Thankfully, my vision was restored, and now by God's grace I see. I didn't sit around and feel sorry for myself, I continued on, business as usual. I didn't throw myself a pity party, and I always say, "If you're going to throw a pity party, don't invite me because I ain't coming." If you believe you too can make it, just like me, say Amen!

CHAPTER 7

LOSING TYRONE AND TYRELL

It's always said that parents are supposed to go before their children but, unfortunately, that's not always the case. We never expect to bury our children. We never even think about it. Your brain can't wrap itself around that fact. It hurts; it hurts every single day, every minute, every time you think about it. You find yourself wondering why it happened. It's the deepest kind of hurt you've ever felt, hurting all the way down in your soul. There's a difference when someone succumbs to an illness. Although it hurts still, you understand what happened and why they died. When someone is murdered, however, there is no understanding. Nothing can explain why there's a sudden gap in your family, why your loved one was here one minute and gone the next. No rhyme, no reason, no explanation. Just calls of condolences, pats on the back, murmurs of "I'm sorry for your loss," or "I know how you feel."

On June 5, 2010, we received a call that no parents want to hear. A somber voice spoke into the phone, "Mr. and Mrs.

Thompson, please come to the hospital right away, it's Tyrone." With dread and trepidation, our family made our way to the hospital, praying all the way. When we got there, we saw Tyrone's friends had beat us there and they were all crying inconsolably. My heart immediately dropped, feeling like it was on a runaway elevator hurtling out of control to the bottom floor of a building.

"What happened?" we asked them, panicking and out of breath. Speaking as a mother, I can assure you that no matter how old and grown your children are, when something's wrong, you run to their rescue. You still want to protect them, care for them, save them, fight their battles for them. You immediately go into "Mama Bear" mode, ready to tackle the world for messing with your cub.

From what we gathered, Tyrone had gone to pick up a friend and while he was sitting in his car waiting in his friend's driveway, two young men approximately eighteen years old came by. The two young men had previously been at a dice game and lost all their money. They told the others they were going to pull a robbery on the first person they ran up on, in an attempt to recoup their money. They saw Tyrone sitting in his car, waiting in his friend's driveway and must've thought he was easy pickings.

Covering their faces, the robbers ran up on Tyrone and although one of them shot him during the course of the robbery, Tyrone managed to shoot them both. They were unaware that Tyrone was actually a former Pagedale police chief. Tyrone was found in the middle of the street with his car engine still running. He'd apparently seen them approaching, and went into "police mode", getting out the car with his weapon not only to protect himself but the general public as well. One of the young men immediately died on the spot from his wounds, but the other survived and was captured when he called the police himself, saying he was a gunshot victim. Upon further questioning, his story was dismantled and he was quickly charged with two counts of second-degree murder, (one count for Tyrone and the other for his accomplice, who died during the commission of the act), first-degree attempted robbery, and armed criminal action. Eventually, he was sentenced to twenty-five years in prison.

I met the surviving man's mother during the trial and she apologized profusely for her son's actions. I told her, "It's not your fault. You can't accept responsibility for your son's actions. I forgive you." We hugged.

Losing Tyrone was hard on all of us. There's still an empty hole in my heart that nothing can fill. Tyrone was a grown man, but he was my baby, my heartbeat. I feel his loss every day and the pain doesn't lessen. There are times when I can remember things about him and smile, but then the sadness that he's no longer with us returns.

Tony kept saying, "He was my best friend. I lost my best friend." Tyrone was Tony's right-hand man, and Tony entrusted him with everything. Tony realized just how much he depended on his brother when the police brought him Tyrone's keys. The key ring was filled with so many keys, Tony had no idea which key opened what. Tyrone took care of everything at KWAME, being responsible for facility maintenance, management for the building group and assets management.

Jack took Ty's death really hard; they were really close and spent a lot of time together, working at the group in security. He doesn't talk about it much, but I can tell how deeply it still bothers him to this day.

Sonja, my daughter, was close to her brother and depended on him for protection, as a little sister always looks up to her big brother. They would go to karaoke together, and he constantly checked in on her. They worked very closely together at the KWAME group.

Kwame, the youngest, was devastated as well. Being that he lived in Atlanta, away from the rest of the family, Tyrone would call his little brother frequently to check on him, give him advice, and just to catch up.

Tyrone was a beloved member of the community, and the community showed how much they loved and appreciated him. They turned out in droves to pay their respects, from citizens to former convicts, community leaders to other law enforcement agencies. Yes, *former* convicts, people he'd arrested came to pay their respects to him. My son loved the people and they loved him right back. Although my son was gone, it touched my heart to see that so many loved my son as I did.

Tyrone was my encouraging child, very nurturing. A week before he was killed, Tyrone turned and suddenly said to me, "Momma, don't ever change, stay as you are." I used to always wonder why he told me that, but I feel he said that because I was always too nice, and people could or would easily take my niceness for naiveté. Many don't know it, but during this time, I was partially blind, having lost my eyesight before going to the State House. Four months later, after Ty's death, my sight suddenly returned. It was as if God gave my sight back, because Tyrone wasn't here to help me, to watch out for me.

Kayla, Tyrone's daughter, went on to get her master's in Education. Tyler, his youngest son, went through a lot of emotional difficulties because of his father's death. Tyrell, his oldest son, went on to become an award-winning artist.

Shortly after Tyrone's death, Tony and his wife Kim, Sonja, Kwame and I started the Tyrone Thompson Institute for Nonviolence. Nonviolent ways of doing things were near and dear to his heart. The Institute takes in kids who are suspended from schools and keeps them, doing homework or studying, instead of sending them home to serve out their suspensions. The Institute also works with troubled teens. This program is truly representative of who Tyrone was. He believed in helping kids and as a police officer, he would often take them home to their parents, instead of just arresting them and putting them into the system. He would give them a good talking to, talk with the parents and try to get through to the child. "Throwing them into the system isn't the answer, if we don't show them the right way to do things."

Tyrone received several awards in his honor:

- Celebrate Family Week – Awarded by Better Family Life.

- Portrait hung by the Beyond the Walls program, sponsored by the Better Family Life organization.

- Placed in the Hall of Fame at University City High School Class of 1982.

***

My grandson, Tyrell, was known to his friends as "Rell Finesse" and was an accomplished artist. He loved cartoons and anime, and never met a stranger. Tyrell was a nurturing role model, and often turned his home and studio into a safe and creative haven for his fellow artists. He loved vibrant colors and stretching his colorful imagination, evident in the art that covered his walls. Always optimistic, even after his father's death, Tyrell would say, "Don't give up on your dreams for St. Louis." He loved his city, the good and bad, and brought out the best in the people he cared about.

Unfortunately, six years later, almost to the exact date of his father's death, we would receive *that* call again. I'd soon learn that my grandson, Tyrell, had met the same fate as his father. Once again, my family had lost a beloved member and was now left with more questions than answers.

On June 8, 2016, Tyrell and a couple of his friends went to an event at a club. As he and a young lady were walking out of the club, they were robbed at gunpoint and Tyrell was shot. The young lady he was with was able to get away unharmed. To date, his murder remains unsolved and we have no closure.

Kayla, who was very close to her big brother, wanted to find a way to not only honor her dear brother's memory, but also to provide a space for artists to inspire their creativity, just as Tyrell had done with his loft. She founded the Finesse Center, located in Jack Thompson Square at 1204 Washington Boulevard. She named it after her brother, as a way to immortalize Tyrell's work and his memory. "This space will provide a place for artists to gather, create, inspire, and work, just as they did at Tyrell's place," she said. The famous "wall" that was in Tyrell's loft was replicated in the Finesse Center. Members of the center have access to computers, printers, art supplies, etc., anything that an artist would need to perfect their craft. There are also seminars, meetings, and forums where the members of the center can receive a discounted admission price to attend.

It's bittersweet that such a beautiful thing came from such a tragic event, but I'm sure if Tyrell were here, he'd be genuinely pleased with the center itself, and the fellowship and amenities it provides to his fellow artists. He'd break into that big wide smile of his and nod.

I made a vow to keep fighting for nonviolence, because this killing has got to stop. We can't blame the police, the system or any of that stuff. We have got to do more with our children, being involved with them, teaching them love and compassion and caring for one another. We know we aren't the only family who's gone through or will go through this. Sadly, a lot of families everywhere have suffered and will suffer, and my heart goes out to them. We must realize that just sitting down waiting for the violence to quietly go away is madness. We must find ways to reach the youth, get them actively engaged in positive things, such as job training and placement, education, and provide positive examples of what being a good member of society and community is like. Until we do that, families will continue to grieve the loss of family members on both sides of the spectrum; death and incarceration.

CHAPTER 8

MY MISSION TO EMPOWER THE COMMUNITY

I've always worked diligently to encourage and empower not only my community, but all communities as a whole, by securing jobs for youth, single moms and heads of households, feeding the hungry, assisting the elderly and encouraging children. I encouraged citizens to know that they mattered, and that I was always dedicated to serving their needs not only while I was in office, but after I retired as well. I've dedicated myself to make sure that citizens know they have not only the right to vote, I encourage them to go and register and actively participate in the election process. If someone decides to run for an elected office, I help them by teaching them the rules, helping them with strategies, and remaining available for advice.

It was and still is my belief that you can't serve a community if you don't show them that you're willing to get in the trenches right alongside them. I was never afraid to "get down and dirty" fighting for what's right, with the people I served. I always considered my constituents my "soldiers" and "leaders" and encouraged them to be my brain, eyes and ears out in the community. I maintained an open-door policy and made sure to answer their calls and messages. Being representative of the people was more than just lip service with me, it was a true calling and one I answered with eagerness, excitement, determination and strength.

I helped found the Black Elected County Officials organization, known as BECO, and was elected co-chair of the organization in 1990. BECO, a non-partisan organization, was founded out of a desire to ensure that black people would have substantial representation in the county government and also in the eighty to ninety cities where they live. I did this because I wanted to help improve the quality of life for all of our county residents. You have to be in the position to get things done. With our organization intact as it is, they can't ignore us anymore. Republicans, Democrats, and Independents listen to the needs of the entire community. The community welcomed us with open arms, believing this is the blanket that could cover all county needs and concerns.

Another endeavor I am proud of was helping Reverend Jesse L. Jackson in three organizations; Operation Breadbasket, PUSH, and the Rainbow Coalition.

CHAPTER 9
HOW TO STAY INVOLVED AS YOU GET OLDER

Stay involved and keep encouraging young people; they are the future. If we aren't active participants and encouragers for them, then who will be? Remember, the Bible says, *"The race is not given to the strong or the swift, but those who endure 'til the end."* Ecclesiastes 9:11

Anything worth having is worth working for. Be the best you can be at whatever you do. Everyone's not cut out to be doctors, lawyers, or engineers. Find out what you're good at and excel at it; everyone has a part to play and can make a difference in this world.

Whatever you do, always remember to give back; it's very gratifying. It's always better to give than to receive. Be a blessing to others whenever you can. I've participated by helping other candidates, giving them advice and by talking to women's groups, organizations, churches and other groups. I've talked extensively to young people, telling them about my story, and reminding them that it's not where you've been, it's where you're going that counts. I try to instill in them a sense of pride, of belonging, of love for their communities, their fellow man and most importantly, themselves.

I'd advise anyone running for office to make sure it's what they want to do. Study the job requirements for that particular office, learn how government works, and take notes on what the expectations are. Make certain you lead by example, because you're always under public scrutiny. You can't just talk a good game; you have to be ready for long hours, hard work, lots of traveling and a serious lack of privacy. Your life is no longer your own, it now belongs to the public, and the public will judge and scrutinize everything you say or do, as well as your family. You have to be accountable and always prepared to answer questions, even when you don't feel like being bothered. It means that you have to be an "open book" and transparent at all times, especially when dealing with expenditures.

Be available to help where you can, wherever and whenever you can. Tony used to say, "I don't understand why people go to jail and use their one phone call to call *my* mother." The answer is quite simple. They call me because they know I'll come to help, even if it means getting out of my bed in the middle of the night. "Mom," he said one day, "I realized they called you because they knew you'd always be there."

Some of my greatest accomplishments have been helping others, teaching, and showing my own kids how to give back. I've always taught my children and grandchildren to reach one, teach one, and never forget where they came from, something I always carried with me.

Staying involved and motivating people doesn't always mean being physical when you get older. Listening and giving some solid advice can also be just as helpful, sharing your experiences and explaining how you solved problems can be beneficial. The younger ones can provide strength, while the elders can provide the wisdom. Working together as a cohesive group can get lots of things accomplished. Never feel that because you're of a certain age that you're "too old" to contribute. In order to get "older", we had to be younger and inexperienced at some point in time. Getting older afforded us the opportunity to see and learn how to do things, how to correct mistakes, and how to achieve success. We're in the prime of our lives and can contribute greatly to our communities by mentoring the younger generation.

Just because I'm retired from politics, that doesn't mean I'm retired from helping. I'll still show up when needed and show out when the situation warrants it. The state of Missouri has term limits, meaning that after eight years, you must step down, to resign if you will. But, although I relinquished my office, I didn't stop going and doing; I don't have a "stop" button. I didn't really consider myself a politician, but more so a community servant. I tried to serve the people, doing things that would best serve the people I represented. I was best in my element when I was helping people or planning how to help them. I'm a community activist, and I will always fight for the rights of *all* people, no matter where they are. In

1988, I was the first African-American woman to be arrested in Washington, D.C., for protesting against apartheid in South Africa. I protested because South Africa was a country where the people didn't have rights, but I've always believed that *all* people have rights. South Africans were finally given their rights in 1994.

Dick Gregory and I did a "Run with Dick Gregory" run, to call attention to homelessness and hunger in the Kinloch, Missouri community, where he was born and raised. And for the record, he actually ran. What most don't know about Dick is that he was a runner, starting in high school. It was during this time that they honored him by naming a street after him. Dick's brother, Ron, happened to be one of my supervisors at HDC.

With Dick Gregory

FINAL THOUGHTS

I've suffered through a lot of grief and tragedy over the years, losing Big Mama, Momma and Daddy, my aunts, six of my brothers and one sister to cancer, my son and grandson, a niece and nephew (my younger sister's children) who died fourteen months apart, and other family members. I pray that no one ever loses loved ones back-to-back like I have. It can get emotionally devastating. Thankfully, through it all, I had my faith in God and my loved ones to see me through it all.

I pray for the turmoil and division in our government to be squashed and that they get back to the business at hand of working for the people, solving the important issues and mending the divisiveness in our country.

I also pray that no one has to suffer from alopecia, but if they do, then I hope they have a strong support system to help them emotionally. I hope that people will learn to see that there's a person behind the lack of hair and accept them for the way they look. I'm looking forward for a day where they either find a cure for it, or that people who have it are treated as if they have a full head of hair.

All my life, I've tried to be a good role model, not only for my husband and children and later on my grandchildren, but for my community, neighbors and others. I've tried to lead by example, always choosing to do the right thing, even when nobody was watching. I've let my conscience be my guide and I've always slept well at night, knowing that I gave the best of me, with everything within me. I've truly represented my people and made the best possible effort to lobby and fight for the things they needed; better education, jobs, housing, healthcare. Some wins, some losses, but I gave it my best shot. Does the system need revamping? Yes, without a doubt. There is still much work to do; the foundation was laid, but the building and renovating never stops. I'm hoping that I've set a model of standards to work by and that someone else can see what I've done and say, "If Ms. Betty can do it, I can do that too."

Someone asked me how I did it all and I told them, it was because I knew God had my back. I struck out on faith, added determination and a willingness to put my all into it. My younger sister, Sandra, would always say that I was her greatest role model, someone she could look up to because I had to be her support system when we lost our parents. I tried to be her support and strength when she lost her two children, Candice and Michael Paul Stittum, less than fourteen months apart. I had the support and love of my family and my community. You'd be surprised what faith and love will do for you. It will propel you to do things you originally thought were completely out of your grasp. There is nothing greater than having someone walk up to you and say, "Thank you. Because of you, I succeeded."

It warms my heart every time someone reminds me that I helped them in some way, whether it was with providing services, finding them jobs or other resources, or just spending some time with them, listening to their issues and allowing them to know their voice was heard.

I can easily say I have no regrets, I honestly don't think I would change a thing about anything I've done with my life. Everything I've done or wanted to do, I accomplished, simply because I had the driven desire to do so. To me, there is nothing better in the world than to say that you've achieved what you've set out to do, setting goals and not only meeting them, but surpassing them as well. Would I do it all again? Yes, I would, without a doubt. How many people can say they worked at doing something they loved? I truly loved working for and with the people; it gave me a sense of gratitude and fulfillment when they achieved their goals, because it meant that I'd also achieved mine.

What do I want people to take away from my book? It is my fervent hope that whoever reads my book is encouraged, inspired and motivated to rise above their own battle scars. Always remember, if you can take it in life, you can make it. I'm living proof that it's true.

Betty L. Thompson

Made in the USA
Monee, IL
28 November 2020